NEW YORK CITY

IN 52 QUOTES

NEW YORK CITY

IN 52 QUOTES

KIT

LESS IS MORE

Ludwig Mies van der Rohe

INTRODUCTION

Flying over the East River, on final
approach to Laguardia Airport, the island
of Manhattan appears surprisingly
compact. It's hard to believe that this sliver
of rock can withstand the weight of the
dreams of untold millions, for nearly four
hundred years.

New York City changes physically,
culturally, and socially nearly every minute.
The 52 quotes in this book help us
understand why its hold on our
imagination, remains unchanged.

- Kit

"NEW YORK HAD ALL THE IRIDESCENCE OF THE BEGINNING OF THE WORLD."

— F. SCOTT FITZGERALD
MY LOST CITY

"LONDON IS SATISFIED, PARIS IS RESIGNED, BUT NEW YORK IS ALWAYS HOPEFUL. ALWAYS IT BELIEVES THAT SOMETHING GOOD IS ABOUT TO COME OFF, AND IT MUST HURRY TO MEET IT."

— DOROTHY PARKER

'GIVE ME SUCH SHOWS - GIVE ME THE STREETS OF MANHATTAN!"

'IT WAS A CRUEL CITY, BUT IT WAS A LOVELY ONE, A SAVAGE CITY, YET IT HAD SUCH TENDERNESS, A BITTER, HARSH, AND VIOLENT CATACOMB OF STONE AND STEEL AND TUNNELED ROCK, SLASHED SAVAGELY WITH LIGHT, AND ROARING, FIGHTING A CONSTANT CEASELESS WARFARE OF MEN AND OF MACHINERY; AND YET IT WAS SO SWEETLY AND SO DELICATELY PULSED, AS FULL OF WARMTH, OF PASSION, AND OF LOVE, AS IT WAS FULL OF HATE."

— THOMAS WOLFE
THE WEB AND THE ROCK

"NEW YORK IS THE MEETING PLACE OF THE PEOPLES, THE ONLY CITY WHERE YOU CAN HARDLY FIND A TYPICAL AMERICAN."

— DJUNA BARNES

"NEW YORK IS THE CONCENTRATE OF ART AND COMMERCE AND SPORT AND RELIGION AND ENTERTAINMENT AND FINANCE, BRINGING TO A SINGLE COMPACT ARENA THE GLADIATOR, THE EVANGELIST, THE PROMOTER, THE ACTOR, THE TRADER AND THE MERCHANT."

— E.B. WHITE

HERE IS NEW YORK

"WE DIDN'T COME
TO NEW YORK TO
STAY SOBER."

— DASHIELL HAMMETT
THE THIN MAN

"WHILE AMERICA WILL ALWAYS, I THINK, FEEL FOREIGN TO ME, NEW YORK CITY IS MY HOME. THIS IS WHERE I CAN CONSTRUCT MY OWN IDENTITY FREELY AND REJECT LABELS IMPOSED ON ME."

— RAQUEL CEPEDA

BIRD OF PARADISE: HOW I BECAME LATINA

'NEW YORK PRESENTED A PARADOX. WHILE FOREIGNERS THOUGHT OF NEW YORK HAS THE SYMBOL OF AMERICA, MANY AMERICANS VIEWED THE CITY WITH SOME SUSPICION AS THE COUNTRY'S MOST FOREIGN.'

— CHARLES EMMERSON

1913: IN SEARCH OF THE WORLD BEFORE THE GREAT WAR

"IF LONDON IS A
WATERCOLOR,
NEW YORK IS AN
OIL PAINTING."

— PETER SHAFFER

"THE BEAUTY OF NEW YORK RESTS ON A COMPLETELY DIFFERENT BASE. IT'S UNINTENTIONAL. IT AROSE INDEPENDENT OF HUMAN DESIGN, LIKE A STALAGMITIC CAVERN. FORMS WHICH ARE IN THEMSELVES QUITE UGLY TURN UP FORTUITOUSLY, WITHOUT DESIGN, IN SUCH INCREDIBLE SURROUNDINGS THAT THEY SPARKLE WITH A SUDDEN WONDROUS POETRY."

— MILAN KUNDERA
THE UNBEARABLE LIGHTNESS OF BEING

"CUT OFF AS I AM, IT IS INEVITABLE THAT I SHOULD SOMETIMES FEEL LIKE A SHADOW WALKING IN A SHADOWY WORLD. WHEN THIS HAPPENS I ASK TO BE TAKEN TO NEW YORK CITY. ALWAYS I RETURN HOME WEARY BUT I HAVE THE COMFORTING CERTAINTY THAT MANKIND IS REAL FLESH AND I MYSELF AM NOT A DREAM."

— HELEN KELLER
MIDSTREAM: MY LATER LIFE

"'NEW YORK!' HE
SAID. 'THAT'S NOT
A PLACE, IT'S A
DREAM.'"

"THE CITY IN WHICH THE SHAPING BY HIS HAND IS MOST EVIDENT IS NEW YORK, TITAN OF CITIES, COLOSSAL SYNTHESIS OF URBAN HOPE AND URBAN DESPAIR. IT HAS BECOME A CLICHÉ BY THE MID-TWENTIETH CENTURY TO SAY THAT NEW YORK WAS 'UNGOVERNABLE,' AND THIS MEANT, SINCE THE POWERS OF GOVERNMENT IN THE CITY HAD LARGELY DEVOLVED ON ITS MAYOR, THAT NO MAYOR COULD GOVERN IT, COULD HOPE TO DO MORE THAN MERELY STAY AFLOAT IN THE MAELSTROM THAT HAD ENGULFED THE VAST METROPOLIS. IN SUCH A CONTEXT, THE CLICHÉ WAS VALID. NO MAYOR SHAPED NEW YORK; NO MAYOR—NOT EVEN LA GUARDIA—LEFT UPON ITS ROILING SURFACE MORE THAN THE FAINTEST OF LASTING IMPRINTS. BUT ROBERT MOSES SHAPED NEW YORK."

— ROBERT A. CARO

THE POWER BROKER: ROBERT MOSES AND THE FALL OF NEW YORK

"WE THOUGHT OF THE PLACE AS A FREE CITY, LIKE ONE OF THOSE STORIED PREWAR TROPICAL NESTS OF INTRIGUE AND LICENTIOUSNESS WHERE EXILES AND LAMSTERS AND REFUGEES FOUND SHELTER IN A TANGLE OF IMPROBABLE JUXTAPOSITIONS."

— LUCY SANTE

LOW LIFE

"EVERYONE IN NEW YORK CITY THINKS THEY ARE FAMOUS WITHOUT BEING FAMOUS."

— ETHAN H. MINSKER

"WHEN I WAS YOUNGER, I HAD WANTED TO BE AT THE VERY CENTER OF ALL THE ACTION IN NEW YORK, BUT I SLOWLY CAME TO REALIZE THAT THERE IS NO ONE CENTER. THE CENTER IS EVERYWHERE - WHEREVER PEOPLE ARE LIVING OUT THEIR LIVES. IT'S A CITY WITH A MILLION CENTERS."

— ELIZABETH GILBERT

CITY OF GIRLS

"ONLY IN A CROWDED, DIVERSE PLACE LIKE NEW YORK, SURROUNDED BY STRANGENESS, DO I COME HOME TO MYSELF."

— JONATHAN FRANZEN
HOW TO BE ALONE

"EACH NEIGHBORHOOD OF THE CITY APPEARED TO BE MADE OF A DIFFERENT SUBSTANCE, EACH SEEMED TO HAVE A DIFFERENT AIR PRESSURE, A DIFFERENT PSYCHIC WEIGHT: THE BRIGHT LIGHTS AND SHUTTERED SHOPS, THE HOUSING PROJECTS AND LUXURY HOTELS, THE FIRE ESCAPES AND CITY PARKS."

— TEJU COLE
OPEN CITY

"IF WHAT MADE AMERICA GREAT WAS ITS INGENIOUS OPENNESS TO DIFFERENT CULTURES, THEN THE SMALL TRIANGLE OF LAND AT THE SOUTHERN TIP OF MANHATTAN ISLAND IS THE NEW WORLD BIRTHPLACE OF THAT IDEA, THE SPOT WHERE IT FIRST TOOK SHAPE."

— RUSSELL SHORTO
THE ISLAND AT THE CENTER OF THE WORLD

"I'D KNOWN SINCE I WAS A CHILD THAT I WAS GOING TO LIVE IN NEW YORK EVENTUALLY, AND THAT EVERYTHING IN BETWEEN WOULD JUST BE AN INTERMISSION. I'D SPENT ALL THOSE YEARS IMAGINING WHAT NEW YORK WAS GOING TO BE LIKE. I THOUGHT IT WAS GOING TO BE THE MOST EXCITING, MAGICAL, FRAUGHT-WITH-POSSIBILITY PLACE THAT YOU COULD EVER LIVE; A PLACE WHERE IF YOU REALLY WANTED SOMETHING YOU MIGHT BE ABLE TO GET IT; A PLACE WHERE I'D BE SURROUNDED BY PEOPLE I WAS DYING TO KNOW; A PLACE WHERE I MIGHT BE ABLE TO BECOME THE ONLY THING WORTH BEING, A JOURNALIST. AND I'D TURNED OUT TO BE RIGHT."

— NORA EPHRON

JOURNALISM: A LOVE STORY

"WHOEVER IS BORN IN NEW YORK IS ILL-EQUIPPED TO DEAL WITH ANY OTHER CITY: ALL OTHER CITIES SEEM, AT BEST, A MISTAKE, AND, AT WORST, A FRAUD."

— JAMES BALDWIN

JUST ABOVE MY HEAD

'WHEN I THINK OF NEW YORK I HAVE A VERY DIFFERENT FEELING. NEW YORK MAKES EVEN A RICH MAN FEEL HIS UNIMPORTANCE. NEW YORK IS COLD, GLITTERING, MALIGN. THE BUILDINGS DOMINATE. THERE IS A SORT OF ATOMIC FRENZY TO THE ACTIVITY GOING ON; THE MORE FURIOUS THE PACE, THE MORE DIMINISHED THE SPIRIT. A CONSTANT FERMENT, BUT IT MIGHT JUST AS WELL BE GOING ON IN A TEST TUBE. NOBODY KNOWS WHAT IT IS ABOUT. NOBODY DIRECTS THE ENERGY. STUPENDOUS. BIZARRE. BAFFLING.'

— HENRY MILLER
TROPIC OF CANCER

"OH I KNOW DARLING, IT'S NOTHING BUT MONEY IN NEW YORK."

— JOHN DOS PASSOS

MANHATTAN TRANSFER

"I HAD NO CONCEPT OF WHAT LIFE AT THE CHELSEA HOTEL WOULD BE LIKE WHEN WE CHECKED IN, BUT I SOON REALIZED IT WAS A TREMENDOUS STROKE OF LUCK TO END UP THERE. WE COULD HAVE HAD A FAIR-SEIZED RAILROAD FLAT IN THE EAST VILLAGE FOR WHAT WE WERE PAYING, BUT TO DWELL IN THIS ECCENTRIC AND DAMNED HOTEL PROVIDED A SENSE OF SECURITY AS WELL AS A STELLAR EDUCATION. THE GOODWILL THAT SURROUNDED US WAS PROOF THAT THE FATES WERE CONSPIRING TO HELP THEIR ENTHUSIASTIC CHILDREN."

— PATTI SMITH

JUST KIDS

'NEW YORK IS NEVER A MEGALOPOLIS OF HOWEVER MANY MILLIONS; IT'S ALWAYS JUST YOUR NEIGHBORHOOD— THE SHOE REPAIR GUY, THE CARPENTER, THE GROCER, THE POST OFFICE—LIKE ANY SMALL TOWN IN TEXAS, REALLY."

"THAT'S HOW NEW YORKERS FEEL," THE DRIVER SAID. "THEY KNOW WHAT BOMBING LOOKS LIKE, AND THEY KNOW THE HELL IT IS. BUT OUTSIDE NEW YORK, PEOPLE WILL FEEL GUILTY BECAUSE THEY WEREN'T HERE. THEY'LL BE YELLING FOR REVENGE OUT OF GUILT AND IGNORANCE. SURE, WE ALL WANT TO CATCH THE CRIMINALS, BUT ONLY PEOPLE WHO WEREN'T IN NEW YORK WILL WANT TO BOMB ANOTHER COUNTRY AND REPEAT WHAT HAPPENED HERE."

— GLORIA STEINEM

MY LIFE ON THE ROAD

"A HUNDRED TIMES
I HAVE THOUGHT:
NEW YORK IS A
CATASTROPHE,
AND FIFTY TIMES:
IT IS A BEAUTIFUL
CATASTROPHE."

— LE CORBUSIER
WHEN THE CATHEDRALS WERE WHITE

"NOW THAT THE NEIGHBORHOOD IS NICE ENOUGH FOR GALLERIES THERE AREN'T MANY ARTISTS LEFT."

— JIMMY WRIGHT

"THEIR CHILDREN, THEIR DOGS, AND HOUSING PRICES: THE HOLY TRINITY OF CONVERSATION FOR NEW YORKERS OF A CERTAIN SORT. FOR THE MEN, THERE WERE ALSO GOLF COURSES AND WINE LISTS TO BE DISCUSSED; FOR THE WOMEN, DERMATOLOGISTS."

— ANNA QUINDLEN
ALTERNATE SIDE

"THE TEN MOST POPULAR KIDS FROM EVERY HIGH SCHOOL IN THE WORLD ARE NOW LIVING IN NEW YORK CITY. THOSE ARE THE PEOPLE WHO MOST OF US WHO CAME TO NEW YORK CAME HERE TO GET AWAY FROM."

— JEREMIAH MOSS

VANISHING NEW YORK: HOW A GREAT CITY LOST ITS SOUL

"HE LOVED THIS CITY. HE HATED IT. IT WAS A CATHEDRAL OF POSSIBILITIES, IT WOULD NEVER SETTLE DOWN, IT MIGHT REMEMBER HIM OR IT MIGHT FORGET HIM, THERE WAS A SENSE OF NO CONTROL…"

— JONATHAN LEE
THE GREAT MISTAKE

"...FOR IN THAT CITY THERE IS NEUROSIS IN THE AIR WHICH THE INHABITANTS MISTAKE FOR ENERGY."

— EVELYN WAUGH

BRIDESHEAD REVISITED

"SO I WENT TO NEW YORK CITY TO BE BORN AGAIN."

— KURT VONNEGUT
BLUEBEARD

"TO EUROPE SHE WAS AMERICA. TO AMERICA SHE WAS THE GATEWAY TO THE EARTH. BUT TO TELL THE STORY OF NEW YORK WOULD BE TO WRITE A SOCIAL HISTORY OF THE WORLD; SAINTS AND MARTYRS, DREAMERS AND SCOUNDRELS..."

— H.G. WELLS
THE WAR IN THE AIR

"SOMEONE NOT FROM NEW YORK SAID THEY HATED IT AND MY ONLY RESPONSE WAS GO HATE YOUR OWN FUCKING CITY / YOU HAVE TO EARN THE RIGHT OF HATING NEW YORK CITY / HAVE YOU"

— PRIYA SOLANKI
CRYING ON THE SUBWAY

"'2.3 MILES AT ITS WIDEST POINT,' WIKIPEDIA CLAIMED, AND JUST 13.4 MILES IN LENGTH. HOW COULD A PLACE SO IMMENSE IN MY DREAMS, SO POWERFUL AND ALIVE, BE SO SMALL?"

— LISA WELDON

TWENTY PIECES: A WALK THROUGH LOVE, LOSS AND MIDLIFE REINVENTION

"HERE I WAS IN NEW YORK, CITY OF PROSE AND FANTASY, OF CAPITALIST AUTOMATION, ITS STREETS A TRIUMPH OF CUBISM, ITS MORAL PHILOSOPHY THAT OF THE DOLLAR. NEW YORK IMPRESSED ME TREMENDOUSLY BECAUSE, MORE THAN ANY OTHER CITY, IT IS THE FULLEST EXPRESSION OF OUR MODERN AGE."

— LEON TROTSKY
MY LIFE

"I WOULD GIVE THE GREATEST SUNSET IN THE WORLD FOR ONE SIGHT OF NEW YORK'S SKYLINE. "

— AYN RAND

THE FOUNTAINHEAD

"THE THING THAT IMPRESSED ME THEN AS NOW ABOUT NEW YORK... WAS THE SHARP, AND AT THE SAME TIME IMMENSE, CONTRAST IT SHOWED BETWEEN THE DULL AND THE SHREWD, THE STRONG AND THE WEAK, THE RICH AND THE POOR, THE WISE AND THE IGNORANT... THE STRONG, OR THOSE WHO ULTIMATELY DOMINATED, WERE SO VERY STRONG, AND THE WEAK SO VERY, VERY WEAK - AND SO VERY, VERY MANY."

— THEODORE DREISER

"A MIDDLE FINGER IS MORE NEW YORK THAN A CORPORATE AMBUSH. I BLEED FOR MY HOMETOWN, AND I'D DIE FOR MY FANS."

— LADY GAGA

"YOU SWALLOW HARD WHEN YOU DISCOVER THAT THE OLD COFFEE SHOP IS NOW A CHAIN PHARMACY, THAT THE PLACE WHERE YOU FIRST KISSED SO-AND-SO IS NOW A DISCOUNT ELECTRONICS RETAILER, THAT WHERE YOU BOUGHT THIS VERY JACKET IS NOW RUBBLE BEHIND A BLUE PLYWOOD FENCE AND A FUTURE OFFICE BUILDING. DAMAGE HAS BEEN DONE TO YOUR CITY. YOU SAY, "IT HAPPENED OVERNIGHT." BUT OF COURSE IT DIDN'T."

— COLSON WHITEHEAD
THE COLOSSUS OF NEW YORK

"NEW YORK WILL BE A GREAT PLACE WHEN IT'S DONE."

— UNKNOWN

"TRUE NEW YORKERS DO NOT REALLY SEEK INFORMATION ABOUT THE OUTSIDE WORLD. THEY FEEL THAT IF ANYTHING IS NOT IN NEW YORK IT IS NOT LIKELY TO BE INTERESTING."

— JIMMY BRESLIN

"THE CITY WAS DIFFERENT BACK THEN-- POOR AND CRUMBLING-- KEPT ALIVE ONLY BY THE GRITTY DETERMINATION AND STEELY CYNICISM OF ITS OCCUPANTS. BUT UNDERNEATH THE DIRT WAS THE APPLE-CHEEKED OPTIMISM OF POSSIBILITY, AND WHILE SHE WORKED, THE WHOLE CITY SEEMED TO THROB ALONG WITH HER."

— CANDACE BUSHNELL

LIPSTICK JUNGLE

"I REGRET PROFOUNDLY THAT I WAS NOT AN AMERICAN AND NOT BORN IN GREENWICH VILLAGE. IT MIGHT BE DYING, AND THERE MIGHT BE A LOT OF DIRT IN THE AIR YOU BREATHE, BUT THIS IS WHERE IT'S HAPPENING."

— JOHN LENNON

"CITIES HAVE SEXES: LONDON IS A MAN, PARIS A WOMAN, AND NEW YORK A WELL-ADJUSTED TRANSSEXUAL."

— ANGELA CARTER

"ONE BELONGS TO NEW YORK INSTANTLY, ONE BELONGS TO IT AS MUCH IN FIVE MINUTES AS IN FIVE YEARS."

— TOM WOLFE

"I ALSO HAD A DIM IDEA THAT IF I WALKED THE STREETS OF NEW YORK BY MYSELF ALL NIGHT SOMETHING OF THE CITY'S MYSTERY AND MAGNIFICENCE MIGHT RUB OFF ON TO ME AT LAST."

— SYLVIA PLATH
THE BELL JAR

"IT COULDN'T HAVE HAPPENED ANYWHERE BUT IN LITTLE OLD NEW YORK."

— O. HENRY

"WHEN YOU LEAVE
NEW YORK, YOU
ARE ASTONISHED
AT HOW CLEAN THE
REST OF THE
WORLD IS. CLEAN
IS NOT ENOUGH."

— FRAN LEBOWITZ

"...QUITE SIMPLY, I WAS IN LOVE WITH NEW YORK. I DO NOT MEAN "LOVE" IN ANY COLLOQUIAL WAY, I MEAN THAT I WAS IN LOVE WITH THE CITY, THE WAY YOU LOVE THE FIRST PERSON WHO EVER TOUCHES YOU AND YOU NEVER LOVE ANYONE QUITE THAT WAY AGAIN."

— JOAN DIDION
SLOUCHING TOWARDS BETHLEHEM

"THE TRUE NEW YORKER SECRETLY BELIEVES THAT PEOPLE LIVING ANYWHERE ELSE HAVE TO BE, IN SOME SENSE, KIDDING."

— JOHN UPDIKE

ABOUT THE AUTHOR

Kit is a reader, writer, listener, and watcher of the human condition. He is the author of the IN 52 QUOTES book series.